10 Commandments for Good Negroes

10 Commandments for Good Negroes
What It Means to be Black and Christian in America

Copyright © 2020 Terrell Carter
Communities Forward Publishing
United States of America

ISBN: 978-0-9792443-2-2
0-9792443-2-3

Cover Design by M. Caldwell- 01 Creative

10 Commandments for Good Negroes:

What it Means to be Black and Christian in America

Table of Contents

Dedication

To Malik and Victoria.

To Genevieve and Jerry Carter for life more abundantly.

Introduction

Since the infamous shootings of Trayvon Martin, Michael Brown, and the like, and professional athletes, such as Colin Kaepernick, taking knees before sporting events to protest perceived police brutality against minorities, our nation has seen an increase in instances where police and citizens have interacted with African Americans in public spaces in not so positive ways. These incidents added more fuel to the public debates about patriotism, nationalism, and the place and importance of race in North American culture.

I live in St. Louis, MO and while the riots and unrest were occurring a few miles away in Ferguson, MO, I heard a consistent refrain from black and white people within the St. Louis

region. That refrain was, "I'm not surprised."
People were not surprised about the racially
discriminatory findings showing how minorities
were treated by various law enforcement
departments in the region, or how municipalities
raised operating funds on the backs of citizens,
or by how political and law enforcement officials
from the region responded with false outrage
and astonishment in the aftermath of the release
of the Department of Justice's comprehensive
report. The racial and economic issues that were
brought to the surface in the aftermath of
Ferguson exemplify the many systems that
sustain the "business as usual" model that is
found in St. Louis and other cities.

One of the things that did surprise me about the
conversations that occurred during the Ferguson
tribulation, although it shouldn't have, was the
participation of white Christians in this process

of vilifying these efforts to bring attention to the experiences and feelings of minority groups who believed that they were once again being held to a different standard for life based on their skin color.

Some of the questions that raised by white Christians were: Why aren't black people more patriotic? Why can't black people just be happy? Why don't black people just follow the rules? These are loaded questions. What do the people who ask these questions mean by the words 'patriotic' and 'happy' or the phrase 'follow the rules', especially when they are asked of people who have not always been considered fully equal to them or their ancestors?

These types of situations and conversations continue to remind the world of the racial and social dysfunction that is uniquely

American. This is why it is important to me to
continue to write about racism and the Church
in America. We tend to think and act like racism,
sexism, and classism no longer exists within the
walls of our faith communities. We pat ourselves
on the back when we have a few families of color
within our communities. I think we would be
better served by acknowledging that our faith
and practice has often served as the beacon for
separation and political jockeying. Instead of
denying the past, we can learn from it so that our
faith can serve as a beacon for love and equality
and living into the principles contained in God's
word.

10 Commandments: What it Means to be Black
and Christian in America seeks to look at what it
takes for black people to be viewed as acceptable
in public spaces by whites, especially white
Christians. The book also seeks to point out long

held unwritten American societal expectations for black people that serve as unofficial guides so that African Americans do not make social or cultural waves. I hope this book spurs open and honest dialogue that will help positively change our nation and the Christian faith we practice in America for our common good and God's glory.

10 Commandments for Good Negroes

1st Commandment

A good negro is patriotic, reveres the flag,
overlooks the sins of his nation, and forgets the
history of his homeland.

2nd Commandment

A good negro is agreeable, agrees to become
what other people expect, agrees that he doesn't
have many options, and lets others agree on
what's best for him.

3ʳᵈ Commandment

A good negro learns the rules and plays by them,
plays by the rules or learns a lesson, plays by the
rules or doesn't play the game, has already
learned a lesson and plays by the rules, and gets
to play because he's learned the rules.

4th Commandment

A good negro is grateful, shows that he's grateful, has a lot to be grateful for, is great at being good, and knows that people are grateful for his goodness.

5th Commandment

A good negro is safe, makes other people feel safe, and brings safety to those who are trying to make him good.

6th Commandment

A good negro doesn't get too close to others, knows the boundaries, graciously stays at a distance, knows why he should keep his distance, and remembers that if he gets too close, he will learn a lesson.

7th Commandment

A good negro has realistic expectations, is careful when keeping things real, doesn't expect good, knows that other people should always be able to expect that he will be a good negro, and allows other people to have high expectations for him.

8th Commandment

A good negro will stay put, puts up with his position in life, puts up and shuts up, and stays within the limitations set for him.

9th Commandment

A good negro doesn't covet a white man's possessions, money, or women, doesn't want what doesn't belong to him, doesn't want what's important to someone else, knows his possessions are secondary to what others want, and understands what's off limits to him.

10th Commandment

A good negro is a good example for other
negroes, finds ways to help other negroes
become good, and learns from the example of
good negroes who have come before him.

A Good Negro Shalt

A Good Negro Shalt Not

11th Commandment

A good negro is not too positive, but is
appropriately positive regardless of what he has
experienced so he can positively fit in.

12th Commandment

A good negro stays in his place, has learned his place and the rules, doesn't step out of his place or push against the rules, and helps other negroes stay in line.

13th Commandment

A good negro is reasonable and so are his expectations.

14th Commandment

A good negro has learned to be content,
compliant and grateful.

15th Commandment

A good negro will only be as happy as you let him be.

16th Commandment

A good negro doesn't let others down, doesn't feel let down by others, and doesn't let his feelings get in the way.

17th Commandment

A good negro works hard to make others feel good, feels good about others, feels good about making others feel good, and feels good being a good negro.

18th Commandment

A good negro is okay with being seen and not heard, being seen but not seen, being heard but not heard, understands that he may be seen but not necessarily heard, and doesn't try to be seen or heard.

19th Commandment

A good negro always acts appropriately, is not proactive, and appropriates the actions and attitudes of the majority appropriately.

20th Commandment

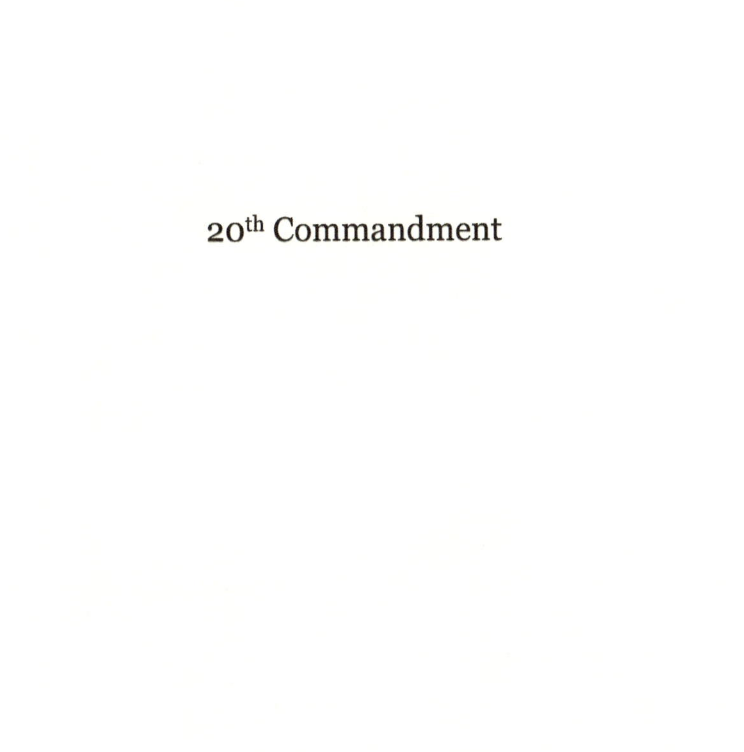

A good negro won't be a positive influence.

21st Commandment

A good negro happily takes what he can get, takes what he is given, doesn't take what's not given to him, is happy with what is taken from him, and is happy to be given anything.

22nd Commandment

A good negro understands that he can't be a prophet while making a profit.

23rd Commandment

A good negro understands that his actions represent his entire race.

24th Commandment

A good negro is a faithful, obedient, compliant
Christian.

25th Commandment

A good negro doesn't move too quickly, neither physically, spiritually, economically, or socially.

26th Commandment

A good negro lives to perform and performs on command.

27th Commandment

A good negro doesn't make waves or allow other negroes to.

28th Commandment

A good negro understands that to make America great again, he must assume his place.

29th Commandment

A good negro internalizes external limitations.

30th Commandment

A good negro is good enough, but not too good.

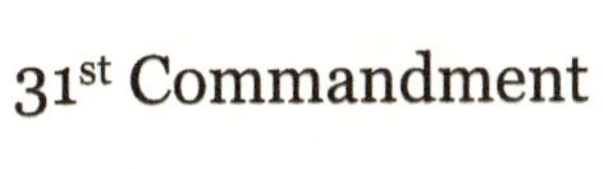

31st Commandment

A good negro can be right but is never the right one.

32nd Commandment

A good negro doesn't hinder others but accepts the hinderances placed on his life.

33rd Commandment

A good negro speaks only when spoken to and
avoids speaking up.

34th Commandment

A good negro knows that education doesn't guarantee opportunity.

35th Commandment

A good negro knows his presence affects property values.

36th Commandment

A good negro knows that the Bible can be a tool
to form other good negroes, knows that the
function of religious faith is to make him into a
good negro, and knows that his faith must
conform to the politics of the majority.

37th Commandment

A good negro knows that his educational attainment isn't enough to make him equal.

38th Commandment

A good negro understands how the world views him, knows where he's welcome and not welcome, understands the limitations of his income bracket, and that when he comes, others will go.

39th Commandment

A good negro is willing to work extra, knows that he needs a strong back, knows the value of physical labor, and is willing to carry the weight of other's expectation.

40th Commandment

A good negro does what's expected, doesn't expect much, expects what's done to him, gets used to others' expectations, and carries the weighty expectations of others.

41st Commandment

A good negro doesn't push back.

42nd Commandment

A good negro understands that freedom is another word for cooperative, and that seeking personal freedom and achievement is akin to being unnecessarily difficult.

A Note to the Reader

You may be wondering why this book does not contain page numbers. During the time that the biblical 10 Commandments was being written, information was recorded in ways completely different from what we are used to. Books, in the sense that we understand them, did not exist. Instead, information was recorded on scrolls. In honor of that, page numbers were not used for this book.

About the Author

Terrell Carter, DMin, is a pastor, professor, and educational administrator from St. Louis, MO. He has served in various ministry positions for over 25 years. He has also worked in higher education for over 20 years. Additionally, he has served as a police officer and nonprofit executive director. You can learn more about him at his website at www.terrellcarter.net or follow him on Twitter and Instagram @tcarterstl.

Upcoming Books from the Publisher:

10 Commandments for Good White Folks